RaC
the driving people

Caring for your bicycle

Your expert guide to keeping your bicycle in tip-top condition

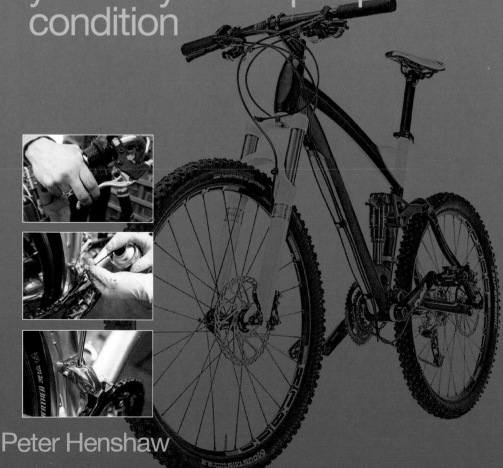

Peter Henshaw

Contents

Renewals
0333 370 4700
arena.yourlondonlibrary.net/
web/bromley

Please return/renew this item
by the last date shown.
Books may also be renewed by
phone and Internet.

RAC
the driving people

Caring for your bicycle

Your expert guide to keeping
your bicycle in tip-top
condition

Peter Henshaw

Also from Veloce Publishing –

www.rac.co.uk
www.veloce.co.uk

This publication has been produced on behalf of RAC by Veloce Publishing Ltd.
The views and the opinions expressed by the author are entirely his own, and
do not necessarily reflect those of RAC. **Please do not undertake any of the
procedures described in this book unless you feel competent to do so,
having first read the full instructions.**

First published in June 2012 by Veloce Publishing Limited, Veloce House,
Parkway Farm Business Park, Middle Farm Way, Poundbury, Dorchester, Dorset,
DT1 3AR, England. ISBN: 978-1-845844-77-6 UPC: 6-36847-04477-0

Fax 01305 250479/e-mail info@veloce.co.uk
web www.veloce.co.uk or www.velocebooks.com.

Readers with ideas for automotive books, or books on other transport or related hobby subjects, are invited to
write to the editorial director of Veloce Publishing at the above address.
British Library Cataloguing in Publication Data – A catalogue record for this book is available from the British
Library.
Typesetting, design and page make-up all by Veloce Publishing Ltd on Apple Mac.
Printed in India by Imprint Digital.

Contents

Introduction & acknowledgements

Introduction

Cycling is a life enhancer; good for you, good for the planet, and great fun. And maintaining your bicycle can be part of that experience. Not only will some simple maintenance and repair jobs keep your bike running smoothly and efficiently, but they will give you extra satisfaction. A bike with under-inflated tyres, a dry chain and slipping gears is not a lot of fun, not to mention hard work to ride. Working as it should, it's a joy.

Bicycles are simple machines, and just a little attention will keep them trouble-free. But even if you would prefer to leave most of this to a bike shop (or a willing member of the family) there are still a couple of jobs – checking brakes and tyre pressures – that all cyclists should be able to do. For safety's sake, it's worth knowing how to spot a faulty brake or tyre, for example.

This book explains how to care for your bicycle, in straightforward language and clear pictures – how to clean it, which tools you'll need, how to make safety checks, do routine maintenance and a few simple repairs. A maintenance schedule outlines how often jobs need doing, and the troubleshooting table should help to pinpoint the cause of any problems. If you are tackling a job you're unfamiliar with, read through the relevant section first, then get to work, with the book by your side.

Hopefully all of this will enable you to get more out of your bike, and maybe use it more often.

Have a good ride.

Acknowledgements

For their help with pictures for this book, thanks go to James Robinson and Eddy at Dorchester Cycles (www.dorchestercycles.org.uk), *A to B* magazine (atob.org.uk), Anna Finch and Bonny Sartin.

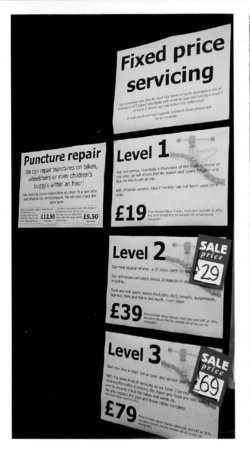

Bike dealers will tackle any jobs you don't want to do, usually at reasonable cost.

Keeping your bike in good shape means you'll get more out of it.

one
Bike basics

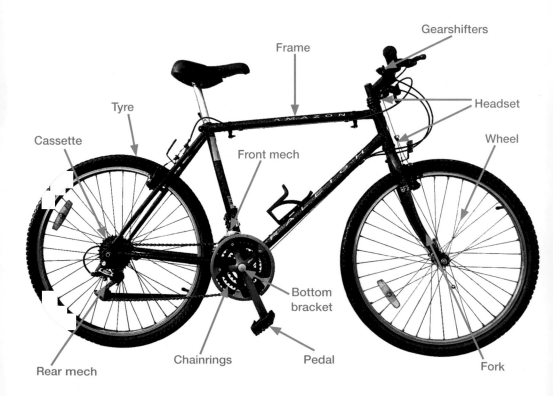

Gearshifters

Frame

Tyre

Headset

Cassette

Wheel

Front mech

Bottom
bracket

Rear mech

Chainrings

Pedal

Fork

What everything does

Frame
Usually steel or aluminium tubing, its job is to support the rider's weight and transfer his/her power through the drivetrain efficiently.

Fork
Needs to absorb road shocks. Telescopic forks on some mountain bikes act as suspension systems.

Pedal
Cheaper pedals are plastic. Clipless metal pedals are more expensive, but transfer power more efficiently.

Chainrings
Two or three of these on a derailleur-geared bike give a wide choice of ratios.

Front mech
Shifts between the chainrings.

Cassette
Cluster of sprockets (from 6 to 9) to give a wide choice of gear ratios.

Rear mech
Shifts between sprockets.

Tyre
Modern tyres deliver a good mix of rolling ability, roadholding and puncture resistance – kevlar bands are sometimes fitted to help ward off punctures.

Wheels
Spoked wheels are relatively light and strong – they very rarely fail.

Gear shifters
Various types, though thumb shifters and twistgrips are most common. Most are indexed, giving one gearchange per click.

Headset
Two sets of bearings allowing forks and handlebars to swivel in the frame, ie steer.

Bottom bracket
Contains an axle on which the pedals are mounted – bottom bracket bearings will need periodic lubrication (unless of the sealed cartridge type), and replacement when worn.

two
Tools

To look after your bike properly, you will need a few tools, even if you are only contemplating the more simple jobs. Some of these – such as spanners, allen keys or pliers – you may already own, but there are also some specialist tools you may need to buy. The good news is that these aren't expensive, and good quality tools, if looked after, will last for years. Your local bike shop should have everything in stock.

The most basic essential item is a pump. The cheapest type clamps onto the frame, but a track pump is worth having at home, as it's far quicker to use and usually comes with a pressure gauge. Puncture repair kits are cheap, and your basic set of tools should also include a set of allen keys (a small multi-set is easier to carry on the bike), spanners and screwdrivers. A spoke key is also a handy tool to have around – having one makes it very simple to tighten a loose spoke.

You don't need to take all of this with you on every ride – carrying unecessary weight is too much like hard work, and tools are rarely needed out on the road. Take the pump, puncture repair kit, a spare inner tube and allen keys, as get-you-home items.

For more involved maintenance jobs, a chain tool is needed to split the chain if it doesn't have a split-link, and for any work on the chainrings or bottom bracket, you will need a crank puller. A cartridge bottom bracket will need a bracket remover, hollow-axle cup tool, and a large slim spanner. To replace inner cables, cable cutters will snip off the cable end neatly.

Bike shops always use a proper workstand, which holds the bike at a comfortable working height. Workstand prices start at around £50, going up to £100 or more – quite an investment, but worth it in the long run if you're looking at doing a lot of maintenance and repairs.

If all of this sounds like too much trouble and expense to purchase all at once, then don't worry. Just gather together the basic items and add to your toolkit as and when you need.

Finally, if your bike is dry, spotless and you have an understanding spouse, it is possible to work on it indoors. But a better solution is a dry and well-lit workshop, whether it's the shed or a corner of the garage, but make sure you aren't cramped.

Basic kit

Pump
Puncture repair kit
Spare inner tube
Allen key multi-tool

Spanners
Screwdrivers
Spoke key

Workshop kit

Basic kit plus:
Track pump
Chain tool
Crank puller
Crank bolt remover
Cassette remover
Chain whip
Hollow-axle cup tool
Hollow-axle crank cap tool
Bottom-bracket remover
Cable cutters
Cable puller
Workstand

Basic get-you-home toolkit.

A track pump inflates tyres quickly and easily.

three
Maintenance schedule

This servicing timetable is a useful guide for planning your maintenance routine. But it's not set in stone – exactly how often your bike needs servicing will depend on how and where it's used. A heavily used mountain bike, or a commuter ridden every day all year round, will need servicing more frequently. A bike ridden only on sunny weekends will need less.

The golden rule is to always keep an eye on things, so that you're always aware when certain parts are nearing the end of their life – see Safety Checks (p23). Brake pads, tyres and wheel rims in particular, should be replaced whenever they are worn or damaged, regardless of the maintenance schedule.

Before every ride

Check the brakes work
Check quick-release levers are secure

Every week

Oil chain and check for wear
Oil jockey wheels
Check crank and chainring bolts for tightness
Check all gears shift accurately
Oil exposed cables
Check inner brake/gear cables for fraying
Check outer brake/gear cables for wear
Check brake pads for wear and alignment
Check brake levers, arms, discs and callipers for cracks

Bikes with suspension only
Check front forks for cracks
Oil front fork stanchion, rear shock body and all seals with teflon oil

Every month

Check sprockets and chainrings for wear

Check bottom bracket for play
Check pedals for play
Oil rear mech pivots and check for
play
Oil inner and outer brake/gear cables
Check hubs for play and
smoothness
Check hub rubber covers for splits

Disc brakes only
Check discs for wear

Bikes with suspension only
Check fork and shock for play
Check all seals for cracks and leaks
Leave bike upside down overnight so
that oil can redistribute in fork

Replace chain (heavily used bikes)
Replace inner brake/gear cables (heavily
used bikes)
Grease open-bearing hubs and check
bearings/surfaces for wear
Grease headset and check for wear
Grease brake bosses
While headset is off, check the fork
steerer tube for cracks

Bikes with suspension only
Replace fork oil
Fork and shock seals should be
replaced every two years, but this is a
specialist job

four
Troubleshooting

This table will help you identify,
understand, and fix common problems.

Chain & gears		
Problem	**Cause**	**Cure**
Chain will not shift onto a smaller sprocket or chainring	Cable is dry or grit has found its way in	Remove inner cable, clean inner and outer with degreaser, lubricate, reassemble
Chain will not shift onto a larger sprocket or chainring	Cable has stretched or front/rear mech out of adjustment	Tighten cable (unclamp at mech end and pull tight), then adjust mech.
Chain jumps on sprockets	Chain and/or sprockets worn, or chain has stiff link; on hub gear bikes, hub may be out of adjustment	If there's a stiff link, free it up; if not replace chain, and if trouble persists, replace sprockets; on hub gear bikes, adjust hub gear
Chain rubs on either side of front mech or (with single chainring) keeps falling off	Bottom bracket worn	Replace bracket cup and bearings (open bearing type) or cartridge (cartridge type)

Brakes		
Problem	**Cause**	**Cure**
Brakes feel sluggish	Cable is dry or grit has found its way in	Remove inner cable, clean inner and outer with degreaser, dry lubricate, reassemble
Long lever travel before brakes work	Stretched cable or worn brake pads	Tighten cable or replace pads
Brake pads do not touch the wheel rim at the same time	Brakes are not centred	Centre the brakes
Brakes are ineffective	The pads are contaminated with grease or a foreign body, or wearing unevenly	Examine pads and remove any foreign body with long-nosed pliers; remove grease or oil with emery cloth; if pads worn unevenly, replace both
Brakes make graunching noise	Grit trapped between pads and wheel rim, or pads severely worn	Clean the pads or replace if worn
Tyres, wheels & steering		
Problem	**Cause**	**Cure**
Bike feels sluggish and hard to ride	Don't blame yourself! The most likely cause is under-inflated tyres	Pump up tyres to correct pressure – you may have a slow puncture; check the tyres again after a few days, and if soft again, you have a puncture
Side to side play at hub	Hub bearings are worn	Replace/adjust bearings
Sudden tinkling noise from wheel	Snapped spoke	Replace spoke
No drive when pedalling	Freehub body is worn. On hub gear bikes, hub out of adjustments	Replace the freehub body or adjust hub gear
Movement at the headset (relative to the bike) when you push bike forwards with front brake applied	Headset worn or loose	Strip and examine the headset – if bearings are worn, replace, regrease and reassemble; if cups and races are worn, take to your bike shop for replacement

Suspension		
Problem	**Cause**	**Cure**
Fork judders when cornering	Rebound is set too fast	Adjust to reduce speed of rebound
Fork often bottoms out	Too light a spring (spring/oil forks) or insufficient air (air/oil forks)	Replaced with heavier-duty spring, or pump in more air, as appropriate
Shock often bottoms out	Insufficient air or over damping	Set up sag on the shock, or adjust damping to speed up the shock's action
Rear wheel lifts under braking	Too much fork dive	Stiffen fork by pumping in more air or increasing pre-load

five
Adjusting the bike to fit you

Adjusting the bike to fit you isn't just about comfort – it will also make your riding more efficient, so you'll be able to ride further with less effort. Riding with the saddle too low, or the handlebars too far away, will make riding harder work than it needs to be.

With one pedal at its lowest point, your leg should be very slightly bent. If you are able to touch the ground with both feet while sitting on the saddle, then the saddle is too low.

Raise or lower the saddle by loosening the seat pin pinch bolt, which may be a quick-release lever or an allen bolt. Retighten and try again. You can also adjust the tilt of the saddle by loosening the allen bolt underneath the saddle.

With the widest part of your foot on the pedal, the depression just behind your kneecap should be directly in line with the pedal axle. If not, move the saddle backward or forward by first loosening the allen bolt underneath the saddle. Loosening this bolt also enables you to tilt the saddle up or down. Some bikes will have a nut and bolt instead of an allen bolt.

Many bikes have brake levers with adjustable reach. If so, adjust so that you can comfortably operate the brake levers with your first two fingers, with the thumb and other fingers holding the handlebars.

Some bikes also have adjustable handlebars. Loosen the allen bolt as shown and swivel the bars to the position you find most comfortable.

19

six
Cleaning

Cleaning is a vital part of caring for your bike, as many components, especially on derailleur gear bikes, are open to the elements and need cleaning of dirt, grit and old lubricant periodically. It's also a good opportunity for a closer look at the brakes, wheels, wheel rims, chain and sprockets, to check that all is well.

Spray degreaser onto the chainset, front and rear mechs, and the chain. If you have one, use a chain cleaning tool as shown here.

Use a stiff brush on the cassette to work in the degreaser, then wash everything in hot soapy water to rinse off the degreaser. Finally, re-lubricate front and rear mechs and chain.

Clean the wheels with a brush and soapy water. This is a very important job – if grit is allowed to build up on the wheel rims, the brake pads will rapidly wear the rim, which can eventually lead to rim failure. Worn aluminium rims can also allow little slivers of metal to become embedded in the brake pads, wearing down the rim even more quickly. If you don't have a workstand, turn the bike upside down by tilting it towards you and gently laying it on its side. Then walk to the other side, grasp the two wheel rims, and lift the bike so that it's resting on the saddle and handlebars. If you have back problems, ask a helper to do this for you.

While the bike is upside down, clean the cable guides under the bottom bracket, and re-lube with a dry lubricant.

Wash the rest of the bike in soapy water, using a sponge or brush so that every crevice is cleaned.

seven
Safety checks

Get into the habit of making routine safety checks, though the only one you need to do before every ride is that the brakes are working correctly.

Push the bike forward with the brakes on. They should prevent the bike moving before the levers reach the handlebars. If the levers do touch the bars, then the brakes need adjusting, or new pads.

With just the front brake on, push the bike forward, feeling for play at the headset.

Standing astride the front wheel, check that the handlebars are straight and tight. If they're not, loosen the clamp bolts or single allen bolt, straighten the bars, and retighten.

Lift the bike (or turn it upside down) and slowly spin each wheel, checking the tyre for serious wear, cuts, splits or bulges. While spinning the wheel, also check for loose or broken spokes.

Check the tyre pressures. Squeeze the tyre walls between finger and thumb – if you can make more than a little impression, the tyre is under-inflated. The recommended pressure should be printed on the tyre wall – road tyres have a higher rated pressure than off-road mountain bike tyres.

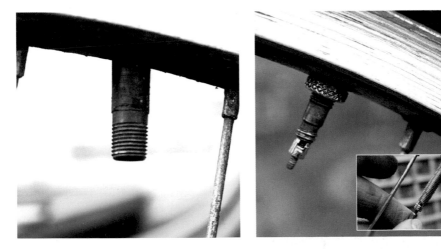

When inflating tyres, note that two different types of valve are used – the fat car-type valve, and the slim cycle-type (which will need the valve tip loosening before inflation; see inset picture). Most pumps have fittings which will accept either type.

25

Check the wheel rims. This is done most easily with a workstand or the bike upside down. If the rims are heavily scored, they need replacing, as they will eventually crack, causing rim failure. Replacing the rim is a job for your bike shop. This rim is in good condition but the tyre needs replacing, due to wear on the sidewall.

Brake and gear cables – check that the inners aren't frayed and that the outers aren't worn. This outer needs replacing.

Check that all other fittings – mudguards, luggage rack, lights – are tight.

Check that all quick-release levers are secure – they should be positioned in line with the fork or frame tube, as shown.

eight
Lubrication

Good lubrication is fundamental to the bike's smooth, efficient running, Without it, the bike will be sluggish and harder work to ride, while the chain, bearings and cables will all wear out far quicker. On the other hand, too much oil on the bike will actually attract dirt and grit. If you have degreaser, use that to remove the old lube first, as this will contain dirt and grit.

Oil the chain after riding in the wet or after cleaning the chain.

The front mech should have light oil applied to the pivots.

Repeat for rear mech pivots and jockey wheels.

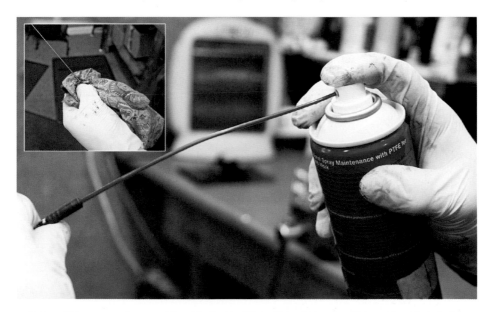

Before fitting a new inner cable, drip light oil into the cable outer. If the old cable is being re-used, remove it, then oil it with the help of a rag (see inset picture) or apply grease. Then refit the inner cable.

On older-type pedals with open bearings, tilt the bike on its side and dribble in some oil.

nine
Adjusting the gears

There's a golden rule regarding gear adjustment – it only needs doing when something is wrong. If the gears are slipping, if the bike is reluctant to change gear or cannot engage the biggest or smallest sprockets or chainrings, then adjustment is needed. The good news is that the drivetrain is far more likely to need a simple adjustment than have developed a fundamental fault.

A note on terminology: 'sprockets' refers to the cluster of cogs at the rear of the bike; 'chainrings' refers to the cogs at the pedals.

Adjusting the front mech

The front mech, located just above the chainrings, shifts the chain from one chainring to another. It does this by moving sideways within set limits (which you can adjust) pushing the chain onto the next chainring. Most bikes will have two or three chainrings.

Shift the chain onto the largest sprocket and smallest chainring. Check that the lower edge of the outer side of the front mech clears the largest chainring – they should be 2mm apart. If the clearance is more or less than that, undo the front mech fixing clamp and raise or lower the mech to adjust it.

Usually, maintenance of the front mech is limited to cleaning out dirt and grit with degreaser, then lubricating it, but if this doesn't cure a shifting problem, then it needs adjusting. The front mech cable runs in a plastic guide under the bottom bracket, which is very vulnerable to dirt – degrease this area, wash it, allow to dry and apply some dry lubricant.

Undo the cable clamp fixing at the front mech. Then screw the low gear adjuster (often marked 'L') in or out until the inner side of the front mech cage is about 2mm from the chain. Pull the gear cable through the clamp and tighten the clamp bolt.

Shift the chain across to the smallest sprocket and largest chainring. Then screw the high gear adjuster (usually marked 'H') in or out to bring the outer side of the front mech cage to about 2mm from the chain. If the mech is failing to shift to the largest chainring, you should need to unscrew the adjuster until you get that 2mm clearance.

Finally, check the front mech is working properly by shifting between all the chainrings – it should shift to each one in turn, quickly and cleanly, and stay on the chainring selected.

Adjusting the rear mech

The rear mech works in a similar way to the front mech, pulling the chain across the cassette to shift to the next sprocket. As with the front mech, it will need degreasing and re-lubing periodically, as it depends on clean movement, free of dirt and grit, to do its job properly. The jockey wheels (the two small cogs below the rear mech) tend to collect dirt, so they too need degreasing and re-lubing regularly.

    If the rear mech won't select the next sprocket, or goes too far and shifts two sprockets at a time, it needs adjusting. As with the front mech you can adjust the outer limits of the rear mech's travel, and also 'fine tune' it to each sprocket with the cable barrel adjuster.

Shift the chain onto the smallest sprocket and biggest chainring, then loosen the cable clamp bolt on the rear mech. Screw the cable barrel adjuster in or out until it is at the halfway position.

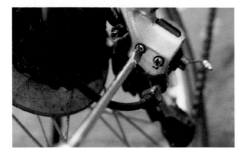

The jockey wheels should be in line with the smallest sprocket. If they're not, screw the high adjuster (usually marked 'H') in or out until they do. Then turn the pedals to check that the chain runs smoothly – if it doesn't, turn the high adjuster in small increments until it does. Pull the cable through the cable clamp and tighten the bolt.

Now shift the chain onto the smallest chainring and largest sprocket. The jockey wheels should be in line with the largest sprocket. If they're not, screw the low adjuster (usually marked 'L') in or out until they are. Then check the chain runs smoothly – if not, tweak the low adjuster again.

Finally, check that the upper jockey wheel isn't making contact with the largest sprocket. If it is, screw in the third adjuster (not the 'L' or 'H' adjuster) as shown.

Adjusting hub gears

Hub gears are a different system to the derailleurs described in the previous pages. Often fitted to town bikes, commuters, folding bikes, and some hybrids, they don't offer the ultra low gears of a mountain bike, and have fewer gears to choose from – usually from three to eight (or 14 speeds on the upmarket Rolhoff system).

Their big advantage is lower maintenance. The gears are sealed away inside the rear hub, thus protected from wet, dirt and grit. Most hub gears have sealed-in lubrication, which doesn't need oiling, and they should last longer than the exposed cassette and front and rear mechs of a derailleur system.

However, they still need care of the shifter cable, and will occasionally need adjustment. If the gears slip, or there's no drive at all in certain gears, then it's adjustment time. This is quite simple, as the only adjustment possible is via the cable. If cable adjustment doesn't do the trick, either the hub satellite is sticking (Shimano Nexus) or the cable itself needs lubrication.

All hub gears operate on the same principle, but the details of adjustment vary from make to make. Sturmey Archer three-speed hubs are found on older bikes and modern folders, while the Shimano Nexus and SRAM systems are the most common on modern full-size bikes. For the details of your hub, refer to the original instructions if you still have them, though the procedures are freely available on the internet.

On Sturmey Archer three-speed hubs, adjustment should be correct when, in gear two, the end of the indicator rod is flush with the end of the inner axle – you can see this though the window in the axle nut, as shown here. If it isn't flush, screw the cable barrel adjuster in or out until it is. Another method, if there is no drive at all in gear two, is to put the hub into gear two. The cable will be slack – undo the cable clamp bolt at the hub gear end and pull the cable through the clamp until it is under very slight tension, then tighten the bolt.

Shimano Nexus three-speed hubs are correctly adjusted when the yellow spot is exactly central between the two yellow lines on the cable box window. If not, screw the cable barrel adjuster in or out until it is.

Shimano Nexus multi-speed hubs use a satellite that can clog with dirt, preventing clean shifting between gears. If this happens, remove the rear wheel by first removing the two axle bolts. To remove the satellite, line up the two yellow dots and remove the lockring. Lift off the satellite and clean it with degreaser, then apply light oil. There is no need to disturb the cable.

Replace the satellite by lining up the yellow triangles on satellite and hub. Then put back the lockring, line up the yellow dots and turn the lockring so that the two dots are separated – the satellite is now locked back into place.

To check gear adjustment, shift to gear four and tilt the bike over (or turn it upside down) until you can see the two red or yellow dots on the gear mechanism. These should be lined up. If they aren't, screw the cable barrel adjuster in or out until they are.

ten

Adjusting the brakes, replacing pads

Properly adjusted and with pads in good condition, your bike brakes will stop you safely and reliably, on wet roads or dry. As with general maintenance, they will need more frequent attention on a mountain bike that sees a lot of off-road use.

If the brake levers need pulling too far before the brakes start working, then the brakes need adjusting – if the levers can be pulled very close to the handlebars, the need is urgent. Also, if the pads are binding – rubbing on the wheel rim when the brakes are off – this too needs attention, as it makes the bike hard work to ride. If the brakes make a graunching noise when used, then there's probably grit trapped between the pad and rim – remove the pads and clean both them and the rims in soapy water. If the trouble persists, replace the pads.

All rim brakes work on the same principle – two brake pads acting on the wheel rim, operated by a cable –

Badly worn brake pad – the bike is dangerous to use with brakes in this condition. Replace pads immediately and check that the wheel rim hasn't been damaged.

but three different types are common: V-brake, cantilever and calliper. V-brakes are the most common, and fitted to many mountain bikes and hybrids. Side-pull calliper brakes, found on some children's bikes, and BMX U-brakes are adjusted in a similar way to calliper brakes. In all cases, check the pads for wear regularly – if they are more than half worn, replace them, and if in doubt, ask your bike shop.

Calliper brake

Adjust the pads so that they are in line with the braking surface on the rim. Then pull on the brake and check that both pads are touching the rim simultaneously – if they're not, use the adjustment screw on the side of the calliper. If the pads are worn, replace them – new pads will come ready-fitted to the shoe.

If there's too much lever travel before the brakes work, undo the cable fixing bolt and squeeze the sides of the calliper until the pads nearly touch the rim, pull the cable through, then retighten the cable fixing bolt. You can fine-tune this adjustment with the cable barrel adjuster, either at the brake end (bottom of the cable) or up at the lever.

V-brake

Unhook the brake cable as shown, then press the brake arms together – they should be vertical when both pads are touching the rim.

If they're not, remove the pads and swap the spacers on either side of the pads around so that they are. If the pads are worn, replace them – new pads will come ready fitted to the shoe, and with all bolts and spacers. Ensure the spacers and washers are assembled in the correct order – make a note of the order when removing the pads.

With the pads back in, hook the cable back into its cradle and check that there's a gap of 1mm between each pad and the rim. To adjust this gap, loosen the cable fixing bolt and pull the cable through until you have a 1mm gap. Then retighten the cable fixing bolt.

Check that the pads are touching the rim simultaneously. If not, screw (in or out) the adjusting screw on each side until they do.

Cantilever brake

Finally, fine-tune the brakes, using the barrel adjuster at the lever, to obtain a shorter lever travel before the brakes work.

Disconnect the brakes by pushing one lever toward the rim, and unhooking the cable. Undo the pivot bolts that attach the cantilever arms to the frame.

Clean the pivots with degreaser, then apply a light grease. Replace the arms and tighten the pivot bolts.

The pads need to be angled-in so that the front of each pad touches the rim before the rear. Loosen the pad fixing bolt and place a piece of cardboard between the rear of the pad and the rim. Apply the brake and tighten the bolt.

Check the pads. Some cantilever pads (not the ones shown) can be replaced separately from the shoe. Remove the spring clip from the shoe, slide out the worn pad, slide in a new one and replace the spring clip. Refit to the cantilever arm, then check that the pad aligns with the braking surface before tightening the bolt.

Finally, adjust the pads by loosening the brake cable clamp bolt and pulling the cable through until there is a 1mm gap between the front of the pads and the rim. Pull the brake lever and check that the pads are touching the rim simultaneously. If they're not, screw (in or out) the centring screws on each arm until they do.

Disc brake

Many mountain bikes now have motorcycle-style disc brakes, either hydraulically or cable operated, giving (especially with hydraulics) more powerful stopping power than a rim brake. Servicing the hydraulic system is a job for the bike shop. Be sure not to contaminate the disc or pads with lubricant – even greasy fingermarks can reduce braking power. Use a specialist disc rotor cleaning fluid. On a cable-operated disc, adjust the lever travel by either loosening the cable clamp bolt and pulling the cable through, or by screwing out the barrel adjuster on the cable.

Carefully inspect the disc rotor for warping by spinning the wheel and examining the rotor end on. If the rotor is warped or cracked it must be replaced – undo the allen or torx bolts holding the disc to the hub, and it will lift off.

The method of replacing disc brake pads varies between models – some pads are retained with a spring; some also have a retaining bolt. These have a simple split-pin. The new pads must be the right ones for your bike, and should click firmly into place.

eleven
Removing/replacing wheels

Several maintainence jobs begin with removing one or both wheels, and the operation is made quicker and easier with quick release levers, which many bikes are now fitted with instead of the traditional axle nuts.

It is essential that the quick release levers are properly locked before the bike is ridden. They should locked in line with the front fork (front wheel) or frame tube (rear wheel), which makes them less likely to be knocked open during a ride. The levers have 'locked' or 'closed' marked on one face, and 'unlocked' or 'open' on the other. When the 'locked'/'closed' face faces outwards, the quick release is locked. Some levers are not marked, but when curved in towards the frame, they are locked. Pushing the lever into the locked position should take some effort.

Before a wheel can be removed, the rim brake will have to be released – this doesn't apply to disc or hub brakes. On V-brakes, unhook the cable from its cradle on the brake arms; on callipers, use the brake's quick release lever; and on cantilevers, unhook the straddle wire from the left brake arm.

Removing the front wheel

Release the brake, pull the quick release lever open (or undo the axle nuts with a spanner) then unscrew the nut on the opposite side enough for the wheel to be taken out.

Lift up the bike and remove the wheel. When replacing the wheel, hand-tighten the quick release nut once the wheel is in place, so that closing the quick release lever requires effort. If the quick release just flops closed easily, it's not secure.

Removing the rear wheel

Shift the chain onto the smallest sprocket. Release the brake, pull open the quick release and loosen the nut opposite. On bikes with axle nuts instead of a quick release, loosen the nuts.

On hub gear bikes, you may need to release the gear cable before the wheel can be removed – the exact method varies from hub to hub, so see the instructions for yours, but you will need to hook the chain off the single sprocket. On derailleur gear bikes, hook the chain out of the way and pull the rear mech backward, then lift up the rear of the bike. The wheel should now drop forward and out of the frame – it may need a slight knock to free it.

To replace the wheel, hook the chain back onto the smallest sprocket (single sprocket on hub gears) before pushing the wheel back into the drop-outs. With the wheel pushed as far back as it will go, and central in the frame (with gear cable reconnected on hub gears), lock the quick release and finally reconnect the brake.

twelve
Punctures

Punctures occur far less often than you might think – you could ride for years and never have one. But they can happen, especially when riding off-road, or on country lanes just after the local farmer has cut the hedges, leaving spiky trimmings all over the tarmac.

Rather than trying to repair a puncture by the roadside, it's far less hassle to fit a new inner tube and repair the punctured tube when you get home. But if you do fit a new tube, carefully check the inside and outside of the tyre for whatever sharp object caused the puncture – fitting a new tube only to have it immediately puncture on the same sharp thorn that caught the first one is no fun.

Remove the wheel and hook the wide end of a tyre lever under the tyre bead. Lever the bead over the rim and hook the other end of the tyre lever round the nearest spoke. Repeat with a second lever, and a third if the tyre is a tight fit on the rim – narrow tyres, and tyres on small-wheeled bikes, can be tougher to remove. Slide one tyre lever around the remainder of the rim until one side of the tyre is off the rim. Then pull out the inner tube, after removing the valve nut (if fitted).

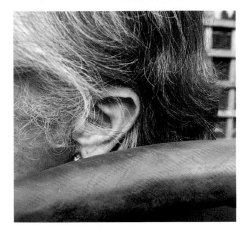

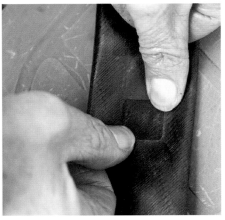

Now inflate the tube a little, hold it up to your ear and listen for the hiss of escaping air. If you can't hear anything, the puncture is a slow one, and the only sure way of spotting it is to immerse the tube in a bowl of water and watch for the telltale bubbles escaping from the leak. When you've found the puncture, mark it with a crayon and let the air out of the tube.

Apply a thin layer of adhesive from the puncture repair kit, using the hole as the centre of the area covered. Leave it a little while to become tacky (not dry) then peel the foil from the back of the patch and press it on firmly, with the centre of the patch over the puncture. Keep applying pressure to the patch for a minute, and make sure the edges are stuck down firmly.

Spread some chalk over the repair to prevent any excess adhesive sticking to the inside of the tyre, and just to be sure, leave the tube for another few minutes so that the adhesive has completely dried.

While the repair is drying, run your fingers over the inside of the tyre to find whatever caused the puncture – be careful, it's likely to be a sharp object! If you can't find anything, it may already have dropped out.

Now it's time to put everything back together. Inflate the tube a little and slip the valve through the hole in the rim, adding the valve nut if there is one (but don't tighten it). Work the tube back inside the tyre, checking that it's not pinched or twisted.

Push the valve upward and work the side of the tyre back over the rim with your fingers, starting with the section next to the valve. Work round the tyre until it is fully on. If the final section is too tough for finger power, use the tyre levers. If it's still reluctant (which can happen with small wheels) a smear of washing up liquid (not oil) on the tip of the rim can do the trick – do wipe all of this off when you're finished.

Fully tighten the valve stem nut (if there is one) then fully inflate the tyre. Refit the wheel, reconnect the brake, and you're done.

thirteen

Accessories

Most new bikes come in very basic form, with no lights, luggage system or mudguards. Fortunately, fitting accessories yourself isn't difficult, doesn't cost an arm and a leg, and makes your bike safer and more comfy to ride.

Mudguards

There's no denying that bikes look sexier without mudguards, which is why so many (not just mountain bikes) are sold without them. But on a wet day they justify themselves many times over, keeping road spray off much of the bike as well as you. They also prevent that embarrassing strip of mud and/or damp up your back.

There are two basic types. The flexible single-fitting type is designed for mountain bikes, giving some protection from spray while keeping maximum clearance to prevent mud clogging. They usually have a simple allen bolt to connect to the seat pin (rear mudguard) and frame front downtube (front mudguard).

Rigid mudguards are only for use on road bikes, and far more effective at keeping you dry. The bike may already have suitable lugs to accept them, but several types will now fit without lugs. But do check that the rigid mudguards you buy suit the wheel size of your bike. If in doubt, ask at the bike shop.

Luggage

How often do you see a cyclist struggling along with a heavy backpack? All that weight high-up makes you less stable, not to mention gives you a sweaty back. The answer is a steel rack and a pair of panniers. Again, the bike shop will advise on which rack will fit your bike. Panniers have come a long way since the days of the traditional touring bag (any colour you like so long as it's black), and there's a big choice of stylish items available. Most are quick release, so they can be unclipped from the bike and taken straight into work or to the shops.

Lights

Bicycle lights have improved hugely in recent years, with LED bulbs giving undreamt of brightness at a fraction of the power consumption of traditional lights. Fitting them is very simple. All come with suitable brackets, and most rear lights attach to the seat pin, front lights to the handlebars. When fitting rear lights, check that they won't be obscured by long jackets or loads on the rack. One other word of warning – don't leave lights on the bike when you park it, as they are easily unclipped and may not be there when you get back!

If you don't want the hassle of changing or recharging batteries, then a hub dynamo is a good investment, especially if you ride every day, all year round. This isn't a cheap option, and as it needs to be built into the wheel with new spokes, is really a job for the bike shop. Probably worthwhile for the all-weather commuter.

Bar ends

Bar ends are well worth fitting to a mountain bike or hybrid. They allow the rider to change position every now and then, improving comfort and ergonomics. To fit them, cut off the end of the existing handlebar grips, slide them on and tighten the pinch bolts.

Bell

A very useful accessory when using a shared use path with pedestrians. A small 'ping' bell will let walkers and other cyclists know that you are approaching from behind, without causing offence. From the walker's point of view, there's nothing more unnerving than to have a bike come up silently from behind and slice past within a hair's breadth. Easily fitted to the handlebars, and make sure the bell is within easy reach, so you don't have to take one hand off the bars to operate it.

Speedometer

Bicycle speedos are more for fun than function, but they do offer a wide array of useful information, including miles ridden, average, current and top speeds, clock, time ridden and even pedal cadence (how fast your legs are spinning). Many are wireless designs that do not need a cable, and can be a very useful aid to training regimes as well as adding interest to the ride.

All speedometers work on the same principle, though some details will differ, and you should refer to the instructions for the exact fitting procedure. Start by fitting the the sensor to the lower fork leg, and the magnet to a wheel spoke, ensuring that the small gap between the two is within the range given in the instructions.

A mirror is a valuable safety aid for riding in traffic. The bar-end type, shown here, gives a clear view and is easy to fit.

Fix the speedometer clamp to a convenient place on the handlebars, where the speedo can be seen easily. Spin the front wheel to check that the speedo has a signal from the wheel sensor, and is working. Finally, you have to programme the speedo to take account of your wheel size – there's usually a table of figures in the instructions which tells you how to do this. Speedos with a cadence sensor will need that fitting as well.

fourteen
Electric bikes

Electric bikes are becoming increasingly popular, as a means of extending your cycling range, helping with hills, or simply making day-to-day cycling easier. Legally, so long as they cannot exceed 15mph under their own power and obey certain weight and power limits, they are treated as a bicycle, so, in the UK, there's no need for a driving licence, tax, insurance or MoT.

As regards maintenance, most of an electric bike's components are the same as those of a conventional bike – brakes, wheels, tyres, gear systems etc – so all the same maintenance procedures apply. The motor of an electric bike is maintenance-free, so no problem there, and if there's a wiring or electronics fault, that's a job for the dealer you bought the bike from, unless you are confident with electrics.

The electric bike's battery, however, will respond to sympathetic ownership, and a few tips will usefully extend its life. These batteries are sealed and do

The battery locks to the bike, but lifts out easily when unlocked.

not use liquid electrolyte, so there is no need to check the levels.

Tips

• Regularly charge the battery, even if you're not using the bike – the worst thing is to leave it low or flat for long periods.

• Don't drop it! The battery might seem very solid, but many contain an electronics pack that is vulnerable to shocks.

• Some battery chargers have a 'refresh' facility, which will fully drain the battery, then slowly recharge it. This evens up the capacity of all the battery cells (which can go out of synch with time). Battery refreshing should be undertaken once a month or so – check the instructions that came with the bike.

• In winter, keep the battery indoors unless you're actually going out for a ride – it will deliver a better range than if kept in a damp, chilly shed.

Charge the battery regularly.

Use the 'refresh' facility – if there is one – once a month or so.

fifteen
More advanced maintenance

Advanced maintenance and repairs are really outside the scope of this book. However, there are several other jobs within reach of the home mechanic, provided she/he has the right tools. What follows is a brief description of each job, and an indication of the tools you will need.

Removing the cassette.

Removing cassette/freewheel

The removal of individual rear sprockets, or the complete cassette and freewheel, requires special tools: a block remover, cassette remover, and chain whip.

To remove the complete cassette and freewheel, remove the rear wheel, and insert the block remover. Untighten the block remover anticlockwise until the cassette lifts off. If individual sprockets are worn, they can be replaced individually on some cassettes. Insert the cassette remover and wrap the chain whip tool around a sprocket. The remover can now be untightened with a spanner. With the cassette's lockring removed, individual spockets can be lifted off.

Replacing brake/gear cables

Replace an inner cable if it has frayed. Undo the clamp bolt at the front mech, rear mech or brake. Gain access to the nipple at the brake lever or gear shifter, and pull the cable out – for gear cables, the chain should be shifted onto the smallest sprocket. Re-use the outer cable if it is in good condition, dribble some light oil into the outers, then thread the new cable through and retighten the clamp bolt.

Replacing chain

Chains do not come in exact lengths, so you will need a chain splitter tool to reduce it to the correct length. Shift to the smallest sprocket and chainring, which makes the chain slack. Split the old chain, remove, and thread the new chain over chainrings, sprockets and through the rear mech. Join the ends of the chain with the splitter tool. With a split-link chain, use long-nosed pliers to remove and replace the split pin.

Greasing wheel hubs

With open bearing hubs, remove the wheel, then remove the locknut on the axle. Pull the axle out. Hook out the ballbearings from both sides of the axle, clean with degreaser, and replace any that are scored or have flat spots. Add grease into the ballbearing groove, press the ballbearings back in and add more grease to hold them in. Replace the axle and tighten the cone until the axle spins freely with no play. Replace the locknut.

Servicing bottom bracket

If there is play in the bottom bracket, and it is a cartridge type, remove both the cranks and use a bottom-bracket remover to draw out the old cartridge. Insert a new cartridge from the drive side. Bottom brackets with open bearings can be greased, as with open bearing hubs. Remove both cranks and axle, then both bearing cups. Degrease and examine the ballbearings, then replace them with fresh grease and reassemble.

Servicing headset

If there is play at the headest when you push the bike forward with the front brake on, it needs servicing. The modern threadless headset is easier to work on than the older threaded type. To gain access to a threadless headset, remove the stem cap bolt, then loosen the pinchbolts on the side of the handlebars, and remove the bars. The forks can now be lowered, giving access to the top and bottom bearings, which should be examined for wear and regreased. Reassemble, finally tightening the stem cap bolt just enough to eliminate play in the headset – if the steering is stiff, you have over-tightened the bolt.

On threaded headsets remove the handlebars after undoing the allen bolt on the steering stem, then use a pair of headset spanners to free the top cup. Lower the forks, watching out for loose ballbearings. Examine the bearings, degrease, then regrease. Tighten the top cup until there is no play but the steering is free, not stiff. Tighten the locknut and, finally, replace the handlebars.

Suspension adjustment

Mountain bike suspension should be adjusted to suit the weight of the rider and the type of riding done. Modern suspension forks are fully adjustable to allow for this. The detail of how to adjust varies between different types of fork, but all should be set up so that the fork sinks by 25 per cent of its full travel when you are sitting on the bike, feet on the pedals. Use pre-load adjustment to alter the amount of 'sag.' Damping controls the speed with which the fork rebounds. Rear shocks have the same range of adjustments. If in doubt, take the bike out and try different settings over the same section of ground, which will give a comparison.

Look after your bike, and it'll look after you.

ISBN: 978-1-845840-95-2
• Paperback • 21x14.8cm • £9.99*
UK/$19.95* USA • 80 pages
• 101 colour pictures

Also available in eBook format

For more info on Veloce titles, visit our website at www.veloce.co.uk
• email: info@veloce.co.uk • Tel: +44(0)1305 260068
* prices subject to change, p&p extra

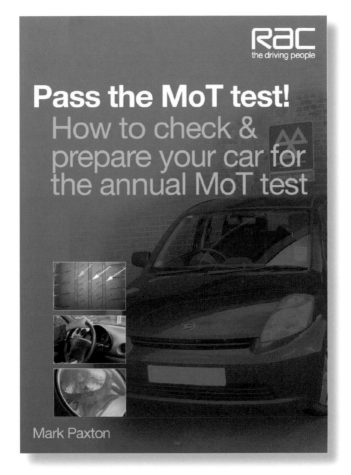

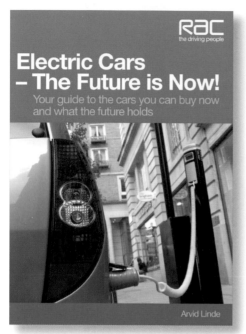

Index